The Mediterranean Diet Cookbook

50 Simple Recipes for a Simple and Delicious Alternative to Healthy Life

The world's best nutrition system,
which allows you to maintain youth and health,
it is useful to everyone without exception.

ISBN: 9781549545641

Table of contents

Introduction

The Mediterranean Diet is perhaps the world's healthiest diet. It is the traditional cooking style of Mediterranean countries which include Southern France, Syria, Italy, Greece, Spain and Egypt. This diet is an abundance of food from natural sources. It incorporates the basics of healthy eating. This diet is largely based on fruits, vegetables, cereal grains, nuts, beans, and olive oil. It includes fish and poultry and lean sources of protein.

Many studies have found that the Mediterranean diet contributes to a lower risk of many fatal diseases. This diet is associated with good heart health. Other studies say it lowers the risk of heart diseases and stroke by up to 30%. It also lowers bad cholesterol, making it less likely to deposit in your arteries.

It is also associated with a reduced risk of cancer, and neurodegenerative diseases such as Parkinson's and Alzheimer's. The researchers noted that women who follow a Mediterranean diet can possibly reduce the risk of breast cancer. It is the ultimate answer if you're looking for a healthy plan to maintain your body and shed pounds.

Philosophy of nutrition:

The Mediterranean diet focuses on healthy foods and the way they are cooked. There is no need to reduce your consumption of food or count calories.

Eat:

Fruits: Apples, oranges, pears, strawberries, bananas, grapes, figs, melon, peaches, dates etc.

Vegetables: Broccoli, kale, tomatoes, spinach, onion, carrots, cauliflower, cucumber, brussel sprouts etc.

Nuts: Almonds, walnuts, cashews, macadamia nuts, hazelnuts.

Seeds: Sunflower seeds, pumpkin seeds etc.

Legumes: Lentils, pulses, chickpeas, beans and peas.

Whole grains: Brown rice, whole oats, corn, whole wheat etc.

Poultry: Chicken, turkey, duck etc.

Seafood: Salmon, tuna, shrimp, oysters, mackerel.

Oil: Extra virgin olive oil

Foods to avoid:

Refined grains: White bread, pasta, spaghetti made with refined wheat etc.

Refine oils: Soya bean oil, cotton seed oil, canola oil etc.

Added sugar: Candies, ice cream, soda etc.

Processed meat and other highly processed food: such as hot dogs, sausages etc.

Eggs and Dairy in moderation and red meat should be eaten rarely.

The Science behind Mediterranean diet:

Scientists and doctors around the world have been researching the Mediterranean diet for more than half a century. It is scientifically proven that people living in Mediterranean countries have very little heart disease compared to Americans.

Scientists and doctors believed that the reason for their low heart disease is a healthy diet i.e. Mediterranean diet.

This diet not only reduces heart disease but also other neurodegenerative diseases such as Alzheimer's, diabetes and more.

Mediterranean Diet Pyramid

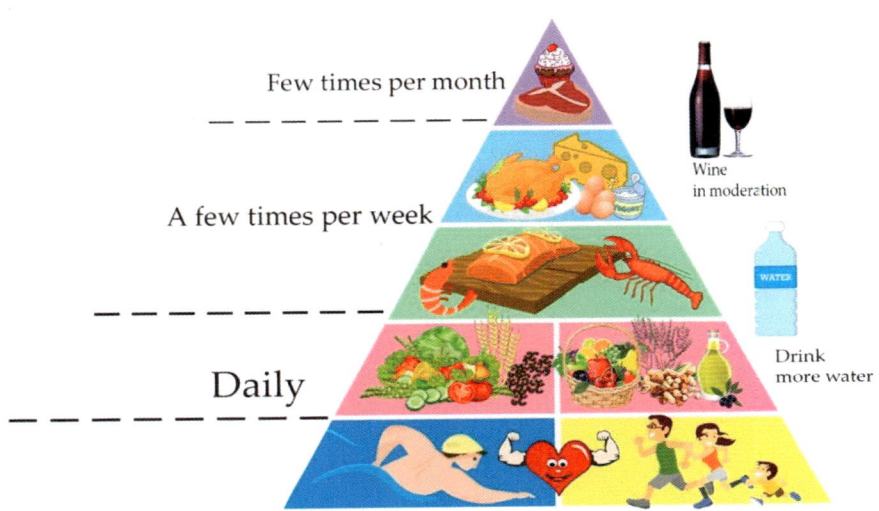

Pyramid:

The fundamentals of the pyramid highlight the importance of food for good health, which leads to a physically active body.

Food items illustrated at the top of the pyramid should be eaten sparingly. The center of the pyramid shows whole foods to be eaten in moderation. The bottom portion of the pyramid reveals the majority of items that should be eaten. All you need to follow a successful Mediterranean diet, is to switch and prepare your brain and yourself for eating more natural and healthy.

Primary products and the diversity of their combinations

Fruits & Vegetables:

Fruits and vegetables are an important staple of the Mediterranean diet. They are the foundation of the Mediterranean diet. Plant based foods are high in vitamins, fiber, antioxidants and minerals. They provide a great amount of energy and promote optimal health. One should eat seven to 10 servings per day. Eating more fruits and veggies significantly reduces the risk of cardiovascular disease, and keeps the bones strong and maintains the cholesterol level as you age. These benefits are amplified with the addition of olive oil.

Olive oil:

Olives and olive oil is the key ingredient most commonly associated with the Mediterranean diet. It is the principal source of the healthy fat. Extra virgin olive oil ranks highest in the category of healthy fat. It helps prevent the formation of blood clots and lowers bad cholesterol i.e. LDL. It boosts the immune system against infection and certain viruses. It promotes good cardiovascular and mental health.

Nut, Seeds and Legumes:

Nuts, seeds, beans and legumes are a good source of protein, healthy fats, and fiber. They contain an excellent amount of antioxidants. They add rich flavor and texture to Mediterranean recipes. They can help slow down digestion and prevent huge swings in blood sugar. They contain large amounts of vitamins B12 and B6, protein, iron, magnesium, zinc and phosphorus. Nuts and seeds such as almonds, hazelnuts, pine nuts, pistachios, sesame seeds and walnuts are high in 'good' unsaturated fat that helps promote weight loss. The quality of calories make them an extremely satisfying food and help you to feel full for a longer time.

Fish and other Seafood:

Fish and other seafood are an important source of healthy protein in the Mediterranean diet. Fish and other seafood such as tuna, sardines, salmon, bream, mussels, clams, shrimp and rainbow trout are rich in Omega-3. In addition to omega-3 they also have nutrients such as zinc, selenium, potassium and iodine - along with Vitamin A which helps to support the immune system, vision and other organs. It also reduces the risk of heart disease.

Dairy & Poultry:

In the Mediterranean diet eggs are greatly appreciated and prepared in scores of ways. Eggs are a good source of protein especially for those who don't eat meat, whereas cheese and yogurt are an important factor for bone and heart health. Chicken and turkey should be cooked using healthy methods, such as roasting, grilling, steaming and baking.

Meat and sweets:

The Mediterranean diet pyramid emphasizes that meat and sweet foods should be eaten sparingly, as they contain high-fat content which makes them an indulgence, not a daily ritual. Meat such as lamb, goat, veal, and beef are enjoyed throughout Mediterranean countries. The fact that daily indulgence of meat is not the norm is what has made the Mediterranean diet so successful. The Mediterranean diet recommends eating less than 1 pound or 455 g of red meat per month. Small servings of sweetened desserts should be eaten in small quantities and consumed less frequently, perhaps as an occasional treat.

Wine:

Wine is the typical drink in the Mediterranean diet. It is associated with social gatherings. It is usually consumed during the main course. It was proved that red wine in moderate amounts increases the health benefits. Moderately means no more than two small glasses of wine daily, preferably with a couple of alcohol-free days during the week. It contains antioxidants and anti-inflammatory properties. It boosts cardiovascular health and promotes brain health.

1: Mediterranean Flat Bread Pizza

Servings: 3

Prep time: 20 minutes   Cooking time: 35-40 minutes

Ingredients:

For Dough:

2 cups whole wheat flour

½ cup luke warm water

2 tablespoons olive oil

1 teaspoon kosher salt

1 teaspoon baking powder

For Sauce:

1 cup tomatoes, chopped

2 garlic cloves, minced

1 tablespoon basil

1 teaspoon oregano

1 teaspoon black pepper

2 tablespoon olive oil

Salt to taste

For Topping:

Kalamata olives

Cherry tomatoes cut in half

Artichoke hearts, chopped

Fresh basil

Feta cheese, crumbled

Olive oil

Directions:

To make the dough:

Mix all the ingredients in a large mixing bowl and knead it until it forms a soft, smooth ball. Let it rest for 10 minutes.

For sauce:

Heat olive oil in a medium saucepan over medium-high heat.

Add garlic and cook for about 1-2 minute, until aromatic.

Add chopped tomatoes and all the spices.

Cover and cook for 10 minutes.

Once cooked and cooled, puree the sauce in a blender.

Assembly:

Preheat oven to 350°F.

Use a rolling pin roll the dough into a 10- to 12-inch rectangle. Transfer to the parchment lined baking sheet.

Brush the flat bread with olive oil all over the top.

Top the bread with a generous amount of sauce, olives, tomatoes, basil and artichokes.

Place in the oven and bake for 8 to 10 minutes until the flatbread is nicely golden and cooked through.

Serve and enjoy.

Nutritional values

Calories 121 kcal

Fat: 6.7 g

Carbs 3 g

Protein 23 g

2: Cucumber Roll Ups

Servings: 4

Prep time: 15 minutes   Cooking time: 10 minutes

Ingredients:

2 large cucumbers

1 carrot, sliced into sticks

1 radish, sliced into sticks

¼ cup hummus

6 tablespoon feta cheese

1 small bunch cilantro

Salt and pepper to taste

Directions

Using a vegetable peeler, shave off long, thin slices of one cucumber.

Cut the carrots, radish and another cucumber into thick sticks.

Pick one cucumber slice and place a teaspoon of hummus, feta cheese, all veggies, some cilantro leaves, salt and pepper.

Start rolling one end of the cucumber slice and roll it around the filling.

Secure the end with a toothpick.

Serve and enjoy.

Nutritional values

Calories 64 kcal

Fat: 5 g

Carbs 3.4 g

Protein 2.5 g

3: Mediterranean Chicken Wings

Makes: 25

Prep time: 2 hours

Cooking time: 40 minutes

Ingredients:

2lbs of chicken wings (about 25)

Celery sticks, for serving

Carrot sticks, for serving

For marinade:

¼ cup olive oil

2 garlic cloves, minced

1 teaspoon dried oregano

1 teaspoon cayenne pepper

1 teaspoon paprika

½ teaspoon salt

Directions:

Mix all the marinade ingredients and refrigerate for half an hour.

Place the chicken wings in a Ziploc bag, add the marinade over the wings and coat evenly.

Seal the bag and refrigerate for an hour.

Take the wings out of the refrigerator about 20 minutes before you plan to cook them so the marinade can soften up a bit.

Preheat oven to 400°F.

Grease a large baking sheet with some olive oil and bake in the heated oven for 30-40 minutes until golden brown and crispy.

Serve with celery sticks and a carrot sticks.

Nutritional values

Calories 283 kcal

Fat: 9 g

Carbs 6.2 g

Protein 16.4 g

4: **Mediterranean Stuffed Capsicum**

Makes: 8

Prep time: 15 minutes

Cooking time: 55 minutes

Ingredients:

8 bell peppers, yellow and red, tops and seeds removed, cored + ¼ cup yellow capsicum, chopped

1lb ground turkey or beef

1 cup short grain rice, cooked

1 onion, finely chopped

1 cup tomatoes, chopped

3 garlic cloves, minced

½ teaspoon hot paprika

½ teaspoon dried oregano

¼ teaspoon freshly ground black pepper

½ cup chopped kalamata olives

¼ cup toasted pine nuts

2 tablespoon olive oil

Salt to taste

½ cup chopped parsley, for garnish

Directions:

Preheat your oven to 350 °F. Grease the baking dish with olives oil.

In a large mixing bowl mix ground turkey, rice, onion, tomatoes, garlic, olives and all the spices.

Place the capsicum into the baking dish.

Fill each capsicum with the mince mixture.

Cover the dish with aluminum foil and bake for 40 minutes or until capsicums are tender.

Remove the foil and bake for an additional 15 minutes, uncovered.

Serve warm and enjoy.

Nutritional values

Calories 198 kcal

Fat: 3 g

Carbs 8 g

Protein 23 g

5: Zucchini Boats

Servings: 6

Prep time: 15 minutes   Cooking time: 20 minutes

Ingredients:

3 zucchini, tops removed, sliced into halves lengthwise

½ cup feta cheese, crumbled

½ cup whole grain croutons (optional)

½ teaspoon garlic powder

3 tablespoon olive oil

1 tablespoon lemon juice

Salt and pepper to taste

Directions:

In a medium pot, bring water to a boil and place the zucchini in the boiling water for 5 minutes. Remove from water and pat dry.

Preheat oven to 350°F and line a baking sheet with parchment paper.

Scoop out the flesh of the zucchini and chop them into chunks.

In a large mixing bowl mix crumbled cheese, garlic powder, olive oil and lemon juice.

Add chopped flesh of zucchini and croutons.

Season with some salt and pepper.

Place the zucchini boat onto the baking sheet and bake for 5-10 minutes until nicely golden brown.

Serve and enjoy.

Nutritional values

Calories 192 kcal

Fat: 14 g

Carbs 8 g

Protein 5 g

6: Shrimp skewers

Servings: 4

Prep time: 30 minutes

Cooking time: 10 minutes

Ingredients:

1 pound shrimp, peeled and deveined

3 garlic cloves, minced

2 tablespoons lemon juice

½ teaspoon crushed red pepper

¼ cup olive oil

Salt to taste

3 tablespoon of chopped coriander, for garnishing

Lemon wedges and cucumber slices, for serving

10-15 wooden skewers

Directions:

Soak the skewers in water.

Place the shrimp in a large mixing bowl.

Add all the ingredients to the shrimp. Toss to coat evenly.

Cover and refrigerate for 30 minutes.

Meanwhile, preheat the grill skillet on medium-high heat.

Add 1 tablespoon of additional olive oil to grill.

Remove the shrimp from the fridge and thread 2-3 shrimp on each skewer.

Grill the shrimps for 5 to 8 minutes, turning over once halfway through.

Place the shrimp on a serving platter and garnish with chopped coriander.

Serve with some fresh lemon wedges and cucumber slices.

Nutritional values

Calories 65 kcal

Fat: 3 g

Carbs 1 g

Protein 3 g

7: Mediterranean Vegetable Soup

Servings: 5

Prep time: 10 minutes

Cooking time: 45 minutes

Ingredients:

2 large zucchini, top removed and sliced

2 carrots, peeled and chopped

2 potatoes, peeled and chopped

1 onion, finely chopped

1 cup tomatoes, diced

1 cup spinach, chopped

1 cup peas

3 sticks celery, finely chopped

1 green bell pepper, chopped

1 liter vegetable stock

2 tablespoon olive oil

3 garlic cloves, minced

1 teaspoon oregano

1 teaspoon black pepper

½ teaspoon turmeric powder

½ teaspoon paprika

½ teaspoon thyme

Salt to taste

Handful of fresh basil leaves, for garnishing

Directions:

Heat olive oil in a pot over medium-high heat, add onion and garlic, stirring well, until they are soft and golden brown.

Add zucchini, carrots, potatoes, tomatoes, spinach, peas, celery and bell pepper.

Cook for 3 minutes.

Add in stock and the remaining spices.

Cover and cook on low for about 45 minutes.

Once cooked, transfer to a serving bowl.

Garnish with some basil leaves and serve with croutons or crusty bread.

Nutritional values

Calories 230 kcal

Fat: 18 g

Carbs 30 g

Protein 27 g

8: Mediterranean Tomato Soup

Servings: 3

Prep time: 10 minutes

Cooking time: 30 minutes

Ingredients:

6 large ripe tomatoes

5½ cups water, chicken broth or vegetable broth

2 sticks of celery

2 tablespoon garlic, chopped

Handful of basil leaves

1 teaspoon oregano

2 tablespoon olive oil

Black pepper and salt to taste

2 tablespoon whipped cream, optional

Directions:

Heat olive oil in a large pan over medium-high heat, sauté onion for 2minutes.

Add tomatoes, celery, oregano, salt and pepper

Cover and cook for 10 to 15 minutes, or until softened.

Add the vegetable broth and simmer for 15 minutes, then puree with a hand blender until nice, smooth and creamy.

Top with a dollop of cream, garnish with fresh parsley and some more ground pepper.

Nutritional values

Calories 290 kcal

Fat: 8 g

Carbs 20 g

Protein 14 g

9: Cauliflower Soup

Servings: 4

Prep time: 10 minutes   Cooking time: 35 minutes

Ingredients:

600 g cauliflower, chopped

2 leeks, finely sliced

4 celery sticks, finely sliced

1 medium onion, finely chopped

1 liter vegetable stock

2 garlic cloves

2 tablespoon olive oil

1 teaspoon turmeric

1 teaspoon oregano

1 small dried chili, chopped

1/3 teaspoon pepper

Salt to taste

Directions:

Heat olive oil in a large sauce pan over medium-high heat.

Add onion and garlic and cook for about 3 minutes until nicely golden brown.

Add the chopped cauliflower, leeks and celery. Cook stirring, for about 5 minutes.

Add the stock, turmeric, oregano, chili, pepper and salt. Simmer for 20 minutes on low heat until vegetables are cooked through.

Once cooked and cooled blend in blender until smooth and creamy.

Return to pan over low heat for 5 minutes.

Serve hot with croutons or your favorite bread.

Nutritional values

Calories 156 kcal

Fat: 10 g

Carbs 38 g

Protein 29 g

10: Seafood Bisque

Servings: 6

Prep time: 10 minutes

Cooking time: 35 minutes

Ingredients:

500g prawns or shrimp, peeled and deveined

300g fish, skinless, cut into 2-inch pieces

1 liter chicken stock

1 onion, chopped

1 carrot, chopped

2 stick celery

1 cup tomatoes, diced

4 garlic cloves, minced

1 dried bay leaf

A pinch of cayenne

Pinch of saffron threads

Salt to taste

Fresh parsley, for garnish

Directions:

Heat the oil in a large saucepan over medium heat.

Add onion and sauté for 5 minutes.

Add minced garlic and cook, stirring, for 2 minutes or until aromatic.

Add chopped carrots, celery, tomatoes and all the spice.

Reduce heat to low and simmer, covered, for 15 minutes or until soup thickens slightly.

Once the soup is thickened remove from heat and let it cool.

Puree in the blender until smooth and creamy.

Put the soup back on the medium-low heat, add shrimps and fish.

Cook for additional 10 minutes.

Ladle the soup among serving bowls and garnish with some fresh parsley.

Nutritional values

Calories 290 kcal

Fat: 20 g

Carbs 38 g

Protein 34 g

11: Pumpkin Soup

Servings: 4

Prep time: 10 minutes

Cooking time: 35-40 minutes

Ingredients:

4 cups pumpkin, diced

2 carrots, chopped

1 onion, finely chopped

2 garlic cloves, finely chopped

2 cups vegetable stock

¼ teaspoon freshly ground nutmeg

1 teaspoon cumin

1 teaspoon ginger, finely chopped

2 tablespoon olive oil

Salt to taste

¼ cup roasted pumpkin seeds, for garnishing

Directions:

In a large pot, heat olive oil over medium heat and sauté onion, garlic and ginger on low heat for about 2 minutes.

Add diced pumpkin and carrots and cook for another 5 minutes.

Add all the remaining ingredients to the pot.

Stir, cover and allow to simmer for about 30 minutes.

Using an immersion blender puree the soup until it's smooth and creamy.

Transfer to serving bowls.

Serve the soup topped with the pumpkin seeds and cream.

Nutritional values

Calories 300 kcal

Fat: 18 g

Carbs 45 g

Protein 23 g

12: Chicken Soup

Servings: 6

Prep time: 15 minutes   Cooking time: 35 minutes

Ingredients:

3lbs chicken

8 cups water

1 onion, chopped

6 carrots, chopped

4 celery stalks, chopped

1 teaspoon black pepper

1 cup fresh parsley, finely chopped

2 tablespoon olive oil

1 lemon, cut into wedges, for serving

Salt to taste

Directions:

In a large pot, heat olive oil over medium heat and sauté onion for 5 minutes.

Add all the ingredients to the pot and bring to a boil.

Reduce heat and simmer, until the chicken is cooked through, about 30 minutes.

Transfer the chicken to a bowl and let it cool.

When the chicken is cool enough to handle, shred the meat and add it back to the soup.

Serve the soup with some fresh parsley leaves and lemon wedges.

Nutritional values

Calories 278 kcal

Fat: 20 g

Carbs 34 g

Protein 43 g

13: Greek Chickpea Soup with Lemon and Olive Oil

Servings: 4

Prep time: 10 minutes

Cooking time: 3 hours

Ingredients:

1 cup chickpeas, soaked 12-18 hours

8 cup water

1 cup spinach, chopped

1 cup tomatoes, chopped

3 tablespoon lemon juice

1 onion, chopped into pieces

1 teaspoon dried parsley

1 teaspoon black pepper

1 teaspoon salt

Fresh parsley to garnish

Directions:

Add all the ingredients to the slow cooker.

Cover and cook for about 3 hours.

Serve the soup hot.

Nutritional values

Calories 352 kcal

Fat: 5.7 g

Carbs 45 g

Protein 9.5 g

14: Zucchini Soup

Servings: 6

Prep time: 10 minutes

Cooking time: 30 minutes

Ingredients:

3 medium zucchini, Sliced

6 cups vegetable stock

1 onion, finely chopped

2 teaspoon garlic, crushed

2 tablespoon olive oil

½ teaspoon thyme

1 teaspoon dried basil

1 teaspoon black pepper

1/2 teaspoon salt

Directions:

Heat oil in a pot over high heat; add onion and garlic, stirring well, until they are soft and golden brown.

Add zucchini and cook for 5 minutes.

Add vegetable stock, thyme, basil, salt and simmer for 20 minutes on low heat until all the ingredients are cooked through.

Once cooked and cooled, blend in blender until smooth and creamy.

Sprinkle some black pepper and serve.

Nutritional values

Calories 145 kcal

Fat: 4 g

Carbs 21 g

Protein 8 g

15: Mediterranean Cucumber Salad

Servings: 3

Prep time: 10 minutes   Cooking time: 5 minutes

Ingredients:

3 cucumber, sliced

½ onion, sliced

2 cups Roma tomatoes, diced

1 cup feta cheese, crumble

1 cup black olives, pitted and sliced

2 tablespoon olive oil, to drizzle

Salt to taste

Directions:

In a large salad bowl, toss all the ingredients together. Chill until serving.

Drizzle some olive oil and serve.

Nutritional values

Calories 131 kcal

Fat: 3 g

Carbs 11 g

Protein 19 g

16: Fattoush Salad

Servings: 4

Prep time: 15 minutes

Cooking time: 5 minutes

Ingredients:

2 loaves pita bread

1 head Romaine lettuce, chopped

1 English cucumber, chopped

5 Roma tomatoes, chopped

5 radishes, thinly sliced

5 green onions, chopped

1 cup fresh parsley leaves, chopped

1 cup fresh mint leaves, chopped

For lime-vinaigrette:

1 lime juice

¼ cup olive oil

½ teaspoon ground cinnamon

¼ teaspoon ground allspice

Salt and pepper to taste

Directions:

Toast the pita bread in oven until it's crisp and nice golden but not browned, break it into pieces.

Meanwhile in a small bowl whisk together all the vinaigrette dressing ingredients.

In another large mixing bowl mix all the veggies.

Add dressing and toss lightly.

Finally, add the pita chips.

Transfer to a serving bowl and enjoy.

Nutritional values

Calories 90 kcal

Fat: 5 g

Carbs 10 g

Protein 2 g

17: Traditional Creamy Hummus

Servings: 4

Prep time: 9 hours

Cooking time: 2 hours 10 minute

Ingredients:

1-1/2 cup chickpeas, soaked overnight

4 tablespoon tahini paste

2 tablespoon yogurt

2 garlic cloves, minced

2 tablespoon lemon juice

Olive oil

Paprika for garnish

Directions:

Place the soaked chickpeas in a medium-sized heavy cooking pot. Add plenty of water and boil for 2 hours.

Once cooked, strain and run under cold water.

Transfer to a large bowl.

Place tahini paste, yogurt, garlic cloves and lemon juice in a food processor. Pulse for few seconds until well combined.

Now add the cooked chickpeas and salt.

Puree until it's smooth and creamy.

Drizzle with olive oil and a dash of paprika and serve with pita bread.

Nutritional values

Calories 166 kcal

Fat: 10 g

Carbs 14 g

Protein 8 g

18: Mediterranean Beets Salad

Servings: 4

Prep time: 10 minutes   Cooking time: 45 minutes

Ingredients:

1lb red beets, thoroughly washed

2 garlic, minced

2 tablespoon lemon juice

2 tablespoon olive oil

A pinch of sea salt

Handful of cilantro, chopped for garnish

Directions:

Place the beets in a large saucepan and add water to cover.

Simmer until tender, about 45 minutes.

Place the beets under running cold water and rinse until beets can be handled.

Peel and chop them into thick chunks.

Add garlic, lemon juice, olive oil, salt and beets to a large mixing bowl.

Mix until well coated.

Garnish with chopped cilantro and serve.

Nutritional values

Calories 105 kcal

Fat: 3.6 g

Carbs 3.5 g

Protein 1.1 g

19: Kidney Bean Salad

Servings: 6

Prep time: 15 minutes   Cooking time: 15 minutes

Ingredients:

2 cups kidney beans, cooked   3 tablespoon olive oil

1 carrot, chopped   2 garlic cloves, minced

1 onion, chopped   3 tablespoon lemon juice

1 cup fresh cilantro, chopped   1 teaspoon paprika

Vinaigrette dressing: Salt and pepper to taste

Directions:

In a large mixing bowl add beans, chopped carrots, onion and parsley.

To make the vinaigrette, whisk all the ingredients together in a small bowl.

Mix the dressing with the beans and vegetable and refrigerate for half an hour.

Serve and enjoy.

Nutritional values

Calories 231 kcal

Fat: 6 g

Carbs 45 g

Protein 18 g

20: Tabouli Salad

Servings: 8

Prep time: 15 minutes   Cooking time: 10 minutes

Ingredients:

3/4 cup extra-fine bulgur wheat

4 Roma tomatoes, finely chopped

1 cucumber, chopped

4 green onion, finely chopped

1 cup fresh parsley, finely chopped

4 tablespoon lemon juice

5 tablespoon olive oil

Salt to taste

Directions:

Wash the bulgur wheat and soak in water for about 10 minutes.

Drain and squeeze the excess water.

Place the chopped vegetables in a mixing bowl.

Add bulgur wheat, lemon juice, olive oil and salt.

Serve with pita or romaine lettuce leaves.

Nutritional values

Calories 202 kcal

Fat: 16 g

Carbs 42 g

Protein 12 g

21: Avocados and Garlic Herb Vinaigrette

Servings: 4

Prep time: 15 minutes   Cooking time: 10 minutes

Ingredients:

3 cups baby Arugula

1 cup cooked couscous

1 avocado, chopped

1 small onion, finely chopped

1 large cucumber, chopped

1 cup Roma tomatoes, halved

1 jalapeno pepper, sliced

4 green onion, chopped

Handful of pumpkin seed, to garnish

Herb Vinaigrette:

½ cup olive oil

¼ cup lemon juice

1 teaspoon rosemary

1 teaspoon oregano

1 teaspoon paprika

1 garlic clove, chopped

2 teaspoon mint, chopped

Salt and pepper to taste

Directions:

In a small mixing bowl, whisk together all the vinaigrette ingredients and set aside.

In another large mixing bowl add all the chopped vegetables and couscous except avocado.

Dress the salad with the vinaigrette and toss until well coated.

Add the chopped avocado and gently mix.

Garnish with some pumpkin seed.

Serve and enjoy.

Nutritional values

Calories 186 kcal

Fat: 10 g

Carbs 29 g

Protein 22 g

22: Mediterranean Tuna Salad

Servings: 4

Prep time: 15 minutes

Cooking time: 20 minutes

Ingredients:

12-ounce can solid white tuna, drained and flaked

1 cup beans, such as chickpeas or kidney beans

½ cup thinly sliced red onion

2 tomatoes, diced

½ cup parsley chopped

1 head romaine lettuce, shredded

15 kalamata olives, pitted

2 tablespoon lemon juice

2 tablespoon olive oil

¼ teaspoon salt

Directions:

Mix chickpeas, onion, tomatoes, parsley and lettuce.

Now add the lemon juice, olive oil and salt to the vegetable.

Add tuna and olives, toss until well combined.

Serve and enjoy.

Nutritional values

Calories 504 kcal

Fat: 23 g

Carbs 44 g

Protein 31 g

23: Slow cooker Chickpea Chicken

Servings: 4

Prep time: 10 minutes   Cooking time 10 minutes

Ingredients:

3lb chicken, cut into pieces, skin removed

1 large onion, finely chopped

3 garlic cloves, crushed

5 medium tomatoes, cut into 1 inch cubes

1 tablespoon ginger, finely chopped

2 cup boiled chickpeas

1 cup kalamata olives, pitted and chopped

1 cup chicken broth, preferably low sodium

2 tablespoon lemon juice

1 teaspoon ground cumin

2 cinnamon sticks

½ cup fresh coriander leaves, chopped

2 bay leaves

1 teaspoon oregano

1 teaspoon black pepper

Salt to taste

Directions:

Add chicken, onion, garlic, ginger, tomatoes, lemon juice and chicken broth to the slow cooker and stir well.

Add the chickpeas, olives and coriander leaves along with all the spices.

Cover and cook on high 4-6 hours until the chicken and veggies are cooked through.

Serve hot with rice.

Nutritional values

Calories 444 kcal

Fat: 8 g

Carbs 29 g

Protein 51 g

24: Turkey Meatballs

Makes 20

Prep time: 15 minutes   Cooking time 30 minutes

Ingredients:

½lb ground turkey

1 medium onion, finely chopped

2 garlic cloves

1 inch piece of ginger, peeled

¼ cup fresh parsley leaves

¼ cup fresh mint leaves

1 tablespoon cumin

½ teaspoon ground cinnamon

½ teaspoon ground black pepper

1 pinch red pepper flakes

2 tablespoon olive oil

½ teaspoon salt

3/4 cup whole wheat bread crumbs

1 large egg, lightly beaten

Directions:

Preheat the oven to 375°F and line a baking sheet with parchment paper.

Mix all the ingredients except oil and onion in a food processor.

Add finely chopped onion and oil to the turkey mixture.

Using your hands work the mixture together; mix until all the ingredients are evenly combined.

Shape the mixture into 12 meatballs and place on the baking sheet.

Bake the meatballs for about 20 to 30 minutes, until the meatballs are golden-brown.

Remove from the oven and cool slightly and serve.

Nutritional values

Calories 376 kcal

Fat: 10 g

Carbs 38 g

Protein 41 g

25: Lemon Chicken with Cucumber Salsa

Servings: 3

Prep time: 10 minutes   Cooking time 6 hours

Ingredients:

For Chicken:

4lb chicken, cut into quarters, skin removed

1 cup chicken stock

1 small onion, finely chopped

3 garlic cloves, crushed

2 tablespoon lemon juice

1 teaspoon paprika

2 teaspoons dried oregano leaves

¼ teaspoon ground black pepper

½ teaspoon salt

2 tablespoons olive oil

2 lemon wedges to serve

For Cucumber and Tomato Salsa:

3 peaches, peeled and diced

1 medium unpeeled cucumber, coarsely chopped

1 tomato, diced

1 tablespoon lemon juice

Directions:

For salsa:

Mix all the diced veggies with lemon juice. Cover and refrigerate until ready to serve.

Add all the ingredients to the slow cooker and cook on low for about 5-6 hours.

Serve the chicken with salsa and lemon wedges.

Nutritional values

Calories 470 kcal

Fat: 6 g

Carbs 7 g

Protein 51 g

26: Greek Chicken Pie

Servings: 8

Prep time: 15 minutes   Cooking time 3 hours-30 minutes

Ingredients:

5 large sheets thawed phyllo dough

1lb chicken breast

1-½ cups chicken broth

½ cup onion, chopped

1 cup potato, peeled and diced

3/4 cup carrot, sliced

1 cup peas

1 tablespoon lemon juice

2 tablespoon olive oil

¼ teaspoon dried thyme

½ teaspoon black pepper

Salt to taste

Directions:

Add all the ingredients to the slow cooker and cook on low for about 3 hours.

Remove the chicken pieces and shred them.

Heat the oven to 375°F.

Meanwhile, roll the dough into a large round.

Pour the filling into deep dish pie plate and cover it with the rolled dough.

With the help of a knife mark 4 slits to let steam escape.

And bake for about 30 minutes until nicely golden brown.

Nutritional values

Calories 480 kcal

Fat: 4 g

Carbs 29 g

Protein 43 g

27: Turkey Burger

Servings: 4

Prep time: 10 minutes   Cooking time 20 minutes

Ingredients:

1lb ground turkey

6 whole-wheat pita breads with pockets, cut in half

½ cup hummus

¼ cup fresh coriander leaves

¼ cup whole-wheat breadcrumbs

1 egg white

2 tablespoon olive oil

2 garlic cloves

1 teaspoon black pepper

1 teaspoon dried oregano

1 teaspoon paprika

½ teaspoon salt

1 cucumber, sliced

1 tomato, chopped into 1 inch chunks

For sauce:

½ cup nonfat plain yogurt

2 tablespoon green chilies, finely chopped

1 teaspoon black pepper

Pinch of salt

Directions:

For yogurt sauce:

Blend all the ingredients in a blender

For Turkey Pattie:

In a food processor mix turkey, coriander leaves, breadcrumbs, egg white, garlic and all the spices. Process until mixed.

Form the turkey mixture into 1 inch thick, 6 oval patties.

Heat the olive oil in skillet over medium heat.

Cook the parties for about 15 minutes or until golden brown.

Fill each pita bread with a turkey Pattie.

Add chopped tomatoes and sliced cucumbers to the pockets.

Serve with yogurt sauce and enjoy.

Nutritional values

Calories 320 kcal

Fat: 7 g

Carbs 17 g

Protein 25 g

28: Lentil Spinach Stew

Servings: 4-6

Prep time: 10 minutes   Cooking time 2 hours

Ingredients:

1-½ cup brown lentils, rinsed

4 cups spinach, chopped

1 medium onion, finely chopped

2 celery sticks, finely sliced

1 carrot, diced

2 garlic clove, crushed

3 cups vegetable stock

2 tablespoon lemon juice

1 teaspoon ground cumin

1 teaspoon red chili powder

2 teaspoon dried mint flakes

1 teaspoon salt

Directions:

Rinse the lentils under cold water until the water runs clear. Place them into the slow cooker.

Add all the veggies, vegetable stock and spices to the lentils.

Cover and cook for about 2 hours.

Serve with boiled rice or crusty bread.

Nutritional values

Calories 210 kcal

Fat: 5 g

Carbs 20 g

Protein 32 g

29: Garlic Beans

Servings: 6

Prep time: 5 minutes   Cooking time: 25 minutes

Ingredients:

½lb dried small white, boiled

2 cups vegetable stock

2 onion, finely chopped

3 garlic cloves, minced

2 large tomatoes, chopped

Handful of fresh basil

1 teaspoon freshly ground pepper

1 tablespoon lemon juice

3 tablespoon olive oil

Fresh coriander, finely chopped

Directions:

Heat olive oil in a heavy skillet.

Add onion and cook for about 2 minutes.

Add garlic, beans, vegetable stock and chopped tomatoes, cover and cook for 15 minutes.

Add basil, pepper and lemon juice, stir and cook for additional 5 minutes.

Once the sauce is thick remove from heat and lets it cool.

Garnish with some fresh corianders and serve.

Nutritional values

Calories 189 kcal

Fat: 8 g

Carbs 30 g

Protein 19 g

30: Chickpea Chili

Servings: 6

Prep time: 15 minutes   Cooking time: 3 hours

Ingredients:

½lb chick peas

3 tomatoes, diced

1 bell pepper, diced

2 cups low sodium chicken broth

1 medium onion

2 garlic cloves

13-15 olives, pitted

1 teaspoon ground cumin

1 tablespoon chili powder

1 teaspoon oregano

1/3 teaspoon ground cinnamon

Fresh parsley and lemon wedges to serve with

Directions:

Heat olive oil in a skillet over medium heat.

Add onion and garlic. Sauté for 5 minutes.

Transfer the cooked garlic and onion to the slow cooker.

Add all the remaining ingredients except parsley.

Cover and cook on high for 3 hours.

Garnish with fresh parsley and lemon wedges.

Serve and enjoy.

Nutritional values

Calories 483 kcal

Fat: 7 g

Carbs 23 g

Protein 39 g

31: Mediterranean Salmon

Servings: 4-6

Prep time: 5 minutes   Cooking time: 30 minutes

Ingredients:

4lb salmon fillets, deboned

Mediterranean Rub:

2 garlic cloves, crushed

1 cup cherry tomatoes

1 tablespoon fresh basil, chopped

2 tablespoon olive oil

2 tablespoon lemon juice

Salt and pepper to taste

Lemon wedges, for serving

Directions:

Preheat oven to 375°F.

In a mixing bowl, mix garlic, tomatoes, basil, oil, lemon juice, salt and pepper.

Rub the salmon with the Mediterranean rub.

Place the salmon on a baking sheet with parchment paper.

Place in the oven and bake for 30 minutes.

Serve with some lemon wedges and enjoy.

Nutritional values

Calories 366 kcal

Fat: 22 g

Carbs 14 g

Protein 29 g

32: Shrimp with Feta Cheese

Servings: 4

Prep time: 10 minutes   Cooking time: 25 minutes

Ingredients:

1-½lb shrimp, peeled and de-veined

1 onion, finely chopped

1 cup tomatoes, diced

2 garlic cloves, crushed

1 cup vegetable or chicken stock

½ teaspoon dried basil

1 tablespoon fresh oregano

2 tablespoons fresh lemon juice

2 tablespoon olive oil

¼ cup feta cheese

Directions:

Heat oil in a large skillet over medium-high heat.

Add onion, garlic and sauté for 5 minutes.

Add tomatoes, vegetable stock and other ingredients.

Add shrimp and simmer for about 20 minutes or until excess liquid evaporates.

Top with feta cheese.

Serve and enjoy.

Nutritional values

Calories 239 kcal

Fat: 12 g

Carbs 24 g

Protein 30 g

33: Sautéed Spinach with Yogurt Garlic Sauce

Servings: 2

Prep time: 5 minutes   Cooking time 10 minutes

Ingredients:

2lbs fresh spinach, thoroughly washed

1 large onion, finely chopped

1 teaspoon ground black pepper

½ teaspoon paprika

5 tablespoon olive oil

2 tablespoons roasted pine nuts

Coarse salt, a pinch

Garlic Sauce:

½ cup plain yogurt

2 garlic clove, crushed

Directions:

Steam the spinach in a steamer basket over boiling water for about 5 minutes.

Meanwhile heat the olive oil in a heavy skillet, cook onion until nice golden, add a pinch of salt.

Add the spinach, and cook, stirring, for 2 minutes. Add nuts and season with black pepper and paprika.

Cook for additional 2 minutes. Remove from the heat and allow cooling at room temperature.

For garlic sauce:

In a small dip bowl mixes together yogurt and garlic.

Transfer the spinach to a serving plate, garnish with roasted pine nuts and top with a dollop of yogurt sauce.

Nutritional values

Calories 179 kcal

Fat: 15 g

Carbs 10 g

Protein 8 g

34: Slow Cooker Butternut Chili

Servings: 2

Prep time: 10 minutes

Cooking time: 4 hours

Ingredients:

2 small butternut squash, peeled and cut into 1/2-inch chunks

½ cup boiled red kidney beans

1 small onion, cut into chunks

½ cup chicken broth

1 apple, cut into 1 inch chunks

¼ cup apple cider vinegar

2 tablespoon brown sugar

1 teaspoon thyme

½ teaspoon black pepper

2 garlic cloves, crushed

3 tablespoon olive oil

Directions:

Place butternut squash, onion, apple chunks beans and all the remaining ingredients to the slow cooker.

Cover and cook for 4 hours on low.

Garnish with some fresh parsley and serve hot.

Nutritional values

Calories 116 kcal

Fat: 4 g

Carbs 21 g

Protein 18 g

35: Roasted Mediterranean Vegetables

Servings: 6

Prep time: 10 minutes   Cooking time 45 minutes

Ingredients:

1 butternut squash, peeled and cut into 1-1/2 inch chunks

3 potatoes, cut into 1-1/2 inch chunks

1 small eggplant, cubed

1 small red onion, cubed

2 garlic cloves, minced

2 tablespoon olive oil

2 tablespoon balsamic vinegar

1 tablespoon fresh, minced thyme

1 tablespoon fresh, minced rosemary

½ teaspoon basil

½ teaspoon oregano

1 teaspoon black pepper

Salt to taste

Directions:

Preheat oven to 300°F.

Grease the roasting dish with non-stick spray or olive oil.

In a small mixing bowl mix all the ingredients except veggies.

Add the veggies in another large mixing bowl and drizzle the dressing over the mixed vegetables, toss well until evenly coated.

Transfer the veggies to the roasting dish and roast them for 45 minutes, rotating the dish after 15 minutes.

Garnish with some fresh rosemary and serve hot.

Nutritional values

Calories 120 kcal

Fat: 3 g

Carbs 18 g

Protein 9 g

36: Mediterranean Eggplant

Servings: 9

Prep time: 10 minutes   Cooking time 50 minutes

Ingredients:

4 small eggplants, sliced

2 tablespoon olive oil

1 cup marinara sauce- recipe follows

Some fresh coriander leaves, chopped

Marinara sauce:

2lb fresh tomatoes, diced

1 large red onion

5 tablespoon tomato paste

4 garlic cloves, crushed

¼ cup fresh basil leaves

¼ cup water

3 tablespoon olive oil

1 teaspoon black pepper

Salt to taste

Directions:

In a large sauce pan, heat olive oil and sauté onion on low heat.

Add all the remaining ingredients to the pan and let it cook for 20 minutes.

Once cooked, cool the sauce completely and blend in the blender until smooth and creamy.

Preheat oven to 300°F.

Spread the sauce in a shallow baking dish and place the eggplant slices in a row.

Drizzle with some olive oil and bake for 30 minutes, until soft.

Garnish with some chopped coriander leaves and serve.

Nutritional values

Calories 150 kcal

Fat: 6 g

Carbs 25 g

Protein 7 g

37: **Mediterranean Zoodle**

Servings: 4

Prep time: 10 minutes   Cooking time 10 minutes

Ingredients:

For Zoodle:

2 large zucchini

2 teaspoon olive oil

For sauce:

300 g cherry tomatoes, sliced in half

1 small onion, finely chopped

1 garlic clove, chopped

15 olives, pitted

3 tablespoon olive oil

Handful of fresh basil leaves

1 lemon juice

½ teaspoon black pepper

½ teaspoon salt

Directions:

For zucchini noodles:

Wash the zucchini and trim the ends off.

Using a spiralizer, create zucchini "noodles."

Heat olive oil in a non-skillet pan.

Place the zoodles into the pan and cook for about 3 to 5 minutes or how tender you prefer the zoodles to be.

For sauce:

Heat olive oil in a small sauce pan and cook onions for 5 minutes.

Add garlic and cook for additional 3 minutes.

Add the remaining ingredients except for olives and mix well.

Mix the zoodles with sauce, add olives.

Garnish with basil leaves and serve.

Nutritional values

Calories 170 kcal

Fat: 8 g

Carbs 19 g

Protein 12 g

38: Roasted Lamb Leg

Servings: 10

Prep time: 10 minutes   Cooking time: 6 hours 45 minutes

Ingredients:

5lb or 2.3 kg of lamb leg
2 cups chicken stock of water
2 onion, sliced into rings
1 head garlic, peeled
2 cinnamon sticks

1 teaspoon rosemary
1 teaspoon oregano
¼ cup lemon juice
4 tablespoon olive oil

Directions:

With the help of sharp knife mark slits in the lamb.

Place the lamb into the slow cooker.

Add all the ingredients over the top of the lamb.

Cover and cook for 6 hours.

Preheat the oven to 350°F.

Remove the leg from the slow cooker and place onto the baking sheet.

Bake for 30 minutes, basting every 15 minutes.

Place the lamb on a serving platter and carve.

Serve warm, with tomatoes and onions spooned over the top.

Nutritional values

Calories 514 kcal

Fat: 32 g

Carbs 8 g

Protein 50 g

39: Herb-Roasted Fish

Servings: 8

Prep time: 10 minutes   Cooking time: 20 minutes

Ingredients:

4 pound bluefish

¼ cup lemon juice

2 garlic cloves, minced

4 tablespoon olive oil

1 red chili, finely chopped

½ teaspoon pepper

½ teaspoon oregano

½ teaspoon rosemary

½ teaspoon thyme

½ teaspoon salt

5 tomatoes, sliced

2 potatoes, sliced

3 carrots, chopped

1 cup spinach, chopped

1 lemon, sliced

Directions:

Preheat the oven up to 375°F and lightly grease a shallow baking dish.

In a small mixing bowl mix lemon juice, garlic, olive oil, red chili, pepper, oregano, rosemary, thyme and salt. Pour the dressing evenly over the fish.

Layer all the chopped vegetables in the bottom of the dish.

Now place the fish over the layered veggies.

Place some sliced tomatoes and lemon on top of the fish and bake for 20 minutes or crispy and golden brown.

Serve warm and enjoy.

Nutritional values

Calories 223 kcal

Fat: 9.8 g

Carbs 2 g

Protein 29.8 g

40: Holiday Mediterranean Pork Chops

Servings: 4

Prep time: 15 minutes

Cooking time: 40 minutes

Ingredients:

4 boneless or bone-in pork loin chops, ½ inch thick

¼ teaspoon freshly ground black pepper

3 garlic cloves, minced

1 tablespoon herbs de Provence

2 tablespoon honey

1 tablespoon olive oil

¼ teaspoon salt

Directions:

Preheat oven to 425°F.

Sprinkle the chops with garlic, salt and pepper, set aside.

In a small mixing bowl combine herbs de Provence, honey and olive oil.

Spread the mixture evenly over all sides of the chops; rub in with your fingers.

Place the chops on a baking sheet, greased with olive oil, roast for 10.

Reduce the oven to 300 F and continue roasting about 30 minutes or juices run clear.

Serve warm and enjoy.

Nutritional values

Calories 161 kcal

Fat: 5 g

Carbs 1 g

Protein 25 g

41: Mediterranean Slow Roasted Duck

Servings: 6

Prep time: 15 minutes   Cooking time: 45 minutes

Ingredients:

1 duck, cut into pieces

For Sauce:

¼ tablespoon tomato paste

3 tablespoon olive oil

¼ tablespoon fresh thyme, chopped

1 teaspoon herbs de Provence

1 teaspoon chili powder

1/3 cup dry white wine

2 tablespoon honey

2 garlic cloves, minced

Salt and pepper to taste

Directions:

Preheat oven to 425°F and grease the baking sheet with olive oil.

In a mixing bowl mix all the sauce ingredients together.

Using your hands generously rub the spices onto each side of the duck pieces.

Place the pieces onto the baking sheet and bake uncovered for 15 minutes.

Cover the duck with aluminum foil and reduce the temperature to 350°F F, bake for additional 30 minutes.

Transfer the duck onto plates and serve with the remaining sauce.

Nutritional values

Calories 472 kcal

Fat: 13 g

Carbs 5 g

Protein 36 g

42: Beef Skewers

Servings: 6

Prep time: 5 hours

Cooking time: 15 minutes

Ingredients:

2lb beef sirloin, cut into cubes

15-20 cherry tomatoes

For marinade:

4 cloves garlic, minced

5 tablespoon olive oil

2 tablespoon fresh lemon juice

1 tablespoon fresh parsley, minced

1 teaspoon dried oregano

1 teaspoon fresh thyme, minced

1 teaspoon fresh rosemary, minced

1 teaspoon lemon zest

½ teaspoon black pepper

Salt to taste

Directions:

Prepare marinade by combining all the ingredients into a large mixing bowl.

Add beef cubes and marinate for 3 to 5 hours.

Preheat the grill to medium-high.

Alternately thread beef and cherry tomatoes onto the skewers.

Brush the beef and tomatoes with oil and grill for 10 to 15 minutes, turning occasionally until the beef is cooked through.

Serve hot.

Nutritional values

Calories 129.8 kcal

Fat: 5.5 g

Carbs 1.7 g

Protein 15.6 g

43: Baklava

Servings: 25-30 pieces

Prep time: 30 minutes

Cooking time: 1 hour 25 minutes

Ingredients:

12-oz phyllo dough, thawed

½ cup pistachio, coarsely chopped

½ cup walnuts, coarsely chopped

¼ cup sesame seeds

¼ cup sugar

2 tablespoon ground cinnamon

A pinch of ground cloves

½ cup butter, for brushing

Syrup:

3/4 cup sugar

1 cup honey

1 cup water

2 tablespoon orange juice   5 whole cloves

1 tablespoon orange zest

Directions:

Preheat the oven to 350°F and grease the baking dish with a bit of the melted butter.

In a large mixing bowl mix all the nuts, sugar, cinnamon and ground cloves.

Roll the dough on a clean surface and make 10 thin sheets.

Brush each layer with butter.

Place 3 layers at a time into the baking dish and layer the generous amount of nut filling, continue until finished with all the layers.

Generously brush the very top layer of phyllo with butter.

Using a sharp knife cut the baklava in diagonal shapes.

Bake on a low rack, for about an hour, until golden and a knife inserted in the center comes out clean.

Meanwhile, prepare the sugar syrup.

In a heavy sauce pan, place water and sugar, occasionally stirring until sugar is dissolved.

Once the sugar is dissolved add honey, orange juice, orange zest and cloves, let simmer for about 25 minutes.

Let the syrup cool at room temperature.

Once the baklava is nice golden, remove from the oven and immediately pour the syrup to cover the entire baklava.

Serve and enjoy.

Nutritional values

Calories 334 kcal   Carbs 29 g

Fat: 23 g   Protein 4 g

44: Walnut Brownies

Makes: 12

Prep time: 15 minutes

Cooking time: 30 minutes

Ingredients:

½ cup all-purpose flour

3/4 cup sugar

1/3 cup cocoa powder

2 eggs

3/4 cup tahini or ¼ cup low-fat yogurt

¼ cup olive oil

¼ teaspoon baking powder

1 teaspoon vanilla extract

1/3 cup walnuts, coarsely chopped

Pinch of salt

Directions:

Preheat the oven to 350°F, Line a 9 inch square pan with parchment paper.

In a small mixing bowl blend, flour, cocoa powder, baking powder, salt and walnuts.

In another mixing bowl, beat sugar and oil together with a beater.

Add eggs and vanilla extract beat again.

Add the flour mixture to the egg batter and mix well.

Fold in the yogurt and mix it again with light hands.

Carefully pour the mixture into the prepared pan and smooth the top with the back of a spoon.

Bake for 30 minutes until a toothpick inserted comes out clean.

Let it cool completely at room temperature.

Cut into squares and serve.

Nutritional values

Calories 200 kcal

Fat: 9.74 g

Carbs 27 g

Protein 4.10 g

45: Pear Tart

Makes: 12-15

Prep time: 15 minutes   Cooking time: 35 minutes

Ingredients:

17 ounce package frozen puff pastry, thawed

3 large pears, washed and sliced

For Syrup:

3 tablespoon sugar

3 tablespoon unsalted butter

A pinch of ground cinnamon

1 tablespoon water

A pinch of salt

Directions:

Heat the oven to 425° F.

On a floured surface, roll out the dough into a thick rectangle.

Using a round cookie cutter, cut 12-15 rounds about 1/8 inch thick.

Place the rounds into the mini tart pan with a removable bottom.

Place the pan in the oven on the middle rack and bake for 30 minutes until crust turns golden brown.

Meanwhile in a small saucepan add water, sugar, butter and cinnamon, bring to a boil, set aside.

Once the puff pastry is nice golden brown, remove from oven and place the sliced pears into the bottom of the pastry.

Drizzle some syrup over the top of the pears and bake again for additional 5 minutes.

Serve warm and enjoy.

Nutritional values

Calories 332 kcal

Fat: 17 g

Carbs 36 g

Protein 6 g

46: Peach Basil Sorbet

Makes: 3

Prep time: 15 minutes   Cooking time: 15 minutes

Ingredients:

3-5 large ripe peaches, chopped and pitted

1 cup sugar

3/4 cup water

¼ cup fresh basil leaves plus more for garnishing

1 tablespoon lemon juice

¼ teaspoon salt

Directions:

Combine sugar, water, salt and basil leaves together in a heavy sauce pan over medium-high heat, bring to boil.

Once the sugar is dissolved, let it stand at room temperature for about 15 minutes.

Meanwhile, cook peaches in a large pot of boiling water for 1 minute.

Pour the syrup through a sieve into a bowl and discard the solids.

Blend the sugar syrup, peaches, lemon juice and salt in a blender.

Transfer the mixture into an airtight container and freeze until firm.

Scoop out the sorbet into the serving glasses, garnish with basil leaves.

Serve and enjoy.

Nutritional values

Calories 121 kcal

Fat: 0.4 g

Carbs 30.6 g

Protein 1.1 g

47: Mediterranean Yogurt Cake

Serving: 10

Prep time: 15 minutes   Cooking time: 55 minutes

Ingredients:

1-½ cup all-purpose flour

1 cup sugar

3 eggs

½ cup olive oil

½ cup low-fat yogurt

2 teaspoon baking powder

1 teaspoon vanilla extract

1 teaspoon orange extract

Pinch of salt

1 teaspoon orange zest

Butter, to grease

Directions:

Preheat the oven to 350°F. Generously grease a loaf pan with the butter.

In a large mixing bowl, mix oil and sugar.

Add eggs and beat again.

Whisk together the flour, baking powder and salt in a separate bowl.

Add the flour mixture to the egg mixture and beat until smooth and creamy.

Add the yogurt, orange zest, vanilla extract, orange extract, beat until completely incorporated in the mixture.

Pour the batter into the pan and bake for 50 minutes or until a toothpick inserted out comes clean.

Serve and enjoy.

Nutritional values

Calories 289 kcal

Fat: 20 g

Carbs 37 g

Protein 5 g

48: Olive oil cookies

Makes: 32

Prep time: 15 minutes   Cooking time: 10-12 minutes

Ingredients:

2-1/4 cups all-purpose flour

1-1/4 cup granulated sugar

1/3 cup olive oil

2 large eggs

½ teaspoon baking powder

½ teaspoon baking soda

3 tablespoon orange or lemon juice

Pinch of rosemary

1 teaspoon vanilla extract

A handful of pine nuts or any other nut of your choice

Directions:

Preheat the oven to 350°F. Lined a baking sheet with parchment paper.

In a mixing bowl, sift together flour, baking powder, baking soda and salt, set aside.

In another mixing bowl, combine sugar and oil, beat until it forms a grainy mixture.

Add in eggs, orange juice, vanilla extract and rosemary, mix until smooth.

Fold in the dry ingredients until just completely incorporated or until forms a soft, sticky dough.

Refrigerate for 20 minutes.

Scoop out the dough and form into 1-inch balls, roll into the sugar to coat.

Sprinkle some nuts over the top of the ball.

Place the cookie balls onto baking sheet and bake for 10 to 12 minutes.

Once puffed and baked, let them cool on a wire rack and serve.

They can be kept in an airtight container for up to a week.

Nutritional values

Calories 120 kcal

Fat: 14 g

Carbs 0 g

Protein 0 g

49: Blackberry Sangria

Servings: 5

Prep time: 8 hours

Ingredients:

750 ml red wine

2 cups blackberries

1 cup orange juice

1 lemon, cut into wedges

1 orange, cut into wedges

Directions:

Add orange juice, blackberries, orange and lemon wedges to the pitcher.

Pour in the red wine, stir and refrigerate overnight for at least 8 hours.

To serve, fill each glass halfway with fruits and then top off with sangria.

Serve and enjoy.

Nutritional values

Calories 262 kcal

Fat: 0 g

Carbs 16 g

Protein 0 g

50: Refreshing Mediterranean Jallab

Servings: 2

Prep time: 10 minutes

Cooking time: 10 minutes

Ingredients:

½ dates pitted

3 cup water

¼ cup raisins

2 tablespoon caramel syrup

Handful of pine nuts

Ice cubes

1 tablespoon rose water

Directions:

Add all the ingredients to the blender, blend until smooth.

Pass the mixture through a sieve and collect the liquid.

Pour the liquid into the serving glasses.

Add ice and garnish with some more pine nuts and raisins.

Nutritional values

Calories 198 kcal

Fat: 0 g

Carbs 19 g

Protein 2 g

Printed in Great Britain
by Amazon